'Classy Chassy'

Ian Logan and Henry Nield

A & W VISUAL LIBRARY · New York

CLASSY CHASSY

American Aircraft 'Girl Art' 1942-1953

This is a book of reproductions of paintings the art historians have missed.

American pop art, which reflected the commercial art-forms of the 1950s and 1960s, had its origins in the World War II boom in mass-production, in machinery and in magazines from which came another, unsung, school of painting: the Girl Art which appeared on U.S. military aircraft of World War II and Korea.

At the same time, Hollywood's dual role in reflecting and influencing American society was particularly apparent in the legends that accompanied the Girl Art. The phrase "Classy Chassy", for example, crops up in the 1940 Raoul Walsh film *They Drive By Night*, in which trucker George Raft is seen leaning on the counter of a diner, remarking on the "classy chassis" of the waitress Ann Sheridan, as he proposes to "finance it". "Who do you think you're kidding?" she sparks back. "Why, you couldn't even pay for the headlights."

Ann Sheridan, known as the "Oomph Girl", was one of the most popular of the Hollywood pin-ups of the period, and though pin-up photographs were used extensively as a source for Girl Art, a letter published in the October, 1943 issue of *Esquire* magazine made it evident that the superb airbrush paintings of Alberto Vargas were firing the creative imaginations of the artists among the ground crews: "As a member of the Armed Forces and away from home, I too am an ardent admirer of a classy 'chassis', such as presented in *Esquire* by the talented Varga. My passion for Varga girls goes almost to the extreme . . ."

In fact, the U.S. Post Office attempted to censor the Varga girls, contending they were "obscene, lewd and lascivious." Varga and verse-writer Phil Stack responded with the famous "Patriotic Gal", decently clad in a nightshirt. The verse declared:

"The American gal
  Is a peach of a pal
    To the boys who are guarding our nation,
  She girds for the fight
  By the yawn's early light
    And her war job is done with elation!
  She always responds
  When she's asked to buy bonds –
    No critic can label HER flighty,
  And because it's in style
  To conserve with a smile
    She's conserving by day and by nighty!"

Subsequently the picture was copied extensively, with varying degrees of finesse (and undress) onto the sides of Flying Fortresses and Liberators in every theatre of operations – becoming one of the most popular Girl Art images of World War II.

Attempts were also made, within the Army Air Force, to censor the Girl Art, but ultimately the paintings were allowed because to have banned them would have posed a serious threat to morale.

At the beginning of American involvement in World War II, "crews of the USAAF would often plaster the Flying Fortresses with drawings and photographs clipped from the pages of *Esquire, Men Only, Look* and similar publications." From this evolved the actual painting onto the aircraft skin, mainly the nose section, though pictures and sweethearts' names were also to be found on the fuselage and tail.

The artists who painted the Girl Art were usually talented members of the ground crew attached to a particular aircraft, some of them having been commercial artists before enlistment. Aircrew members also painted, or had painted for them, pictures of wives and sweethearts on their leather A-2 jackets, the protective and personalizing effect of Girl Art not being restricted to the aircraft. It is interesting to note the recurrence of the same image on different aircraft and jackets, some pin-ups obviously lending themselves more to the task in hand.

Girl Art painting developed in expertise with the increasing number of aircraft being deployed in Europe and the Pacific, and by the end of World War II (and also in the Korean War) the demand had created a small industry for the best artists, one of them being paid $15 per aircraft, with a whole squadron on his books. Generally speaking, the work of these artists was more polished, and perhaps slightly less personal, than the one-off commissions that produced the earlier examples of Girl Art.

By the onset of the Korean War, Girl Art had lost its virginity, moving with the times to the less romantic imagery of the 1950s, when the girlie magazines and pin-up calendars became more explicit in their appeal.

During the U.S. Air Force's involvement in Vietnam, Girl Art as such did not exist, though there was one example worth mentioning. An F105D "Thunderchief" had a large nude painted prominently on the nose "to help" in the words of the artist and pilot, "the refueling boomer (of the airtanker) improve his aim and add a little humor to the war effort." The plane's name? "Pussy Galor".

The purpose of this collection of pictures then is to give an art-form that was thrown up at a time of crisis, a chance to be seen and remembered. Girl Art was, for the average American airman in the 1940s, a personal form of expression not catered for in the official squadron insignia. Whatever sexual fantasies the pin-up pictures may have provided for him, the Girl Art painted on his aircraft imbued that mass-produced piece of flying machinery with a personality no serial number could ever give.

Henry Nield

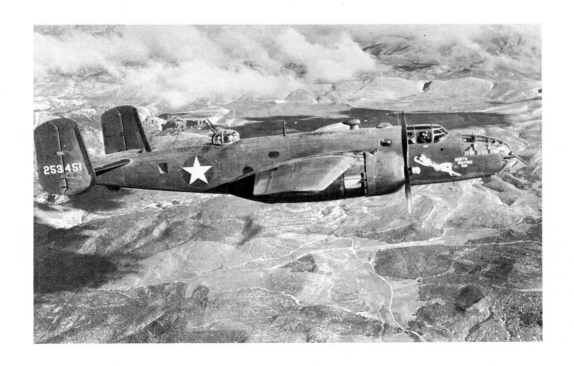

B25 Mitchell 'Worth Fighting For' over Italy 1944 (*USAF*). *Front Cover* 'Sleepy Time Gal', section-B24 Liberator (*CAF Collection*).

Above 'Sack Time', section-B24 Liberator (*CAF Collection*). *Opposite* Varga's 'Patriotic Gal', pin-up (© *1944 Esquire Inc.*).

PATRIOTIC GAL

The American gal
Is a peach of a pal
To the boys who are guarding our nation,
She girds for the fight
By the yawn's early light
And her war job is done with elation!
She always responds
When she's asked to buy bonds—
No critic can label HER flighty,
And because it's in style
To conserve with a smile
She's conserving by day and by nighty!

PAINTING BY VARGA
VERSE BY PHIL STACK

Opposite 'O O Nothing', section-B24 Liberator (*CAF Collection*). *Above* 'Night Mission', B24 Liberator, Guam, Marianas Islands, 1944 (*USAF*).

Above 'Double Trouble', section-B24 Liberator (*CAF Collection*). *Opposite* Twin-engine B26 Marauder (*USAF*).

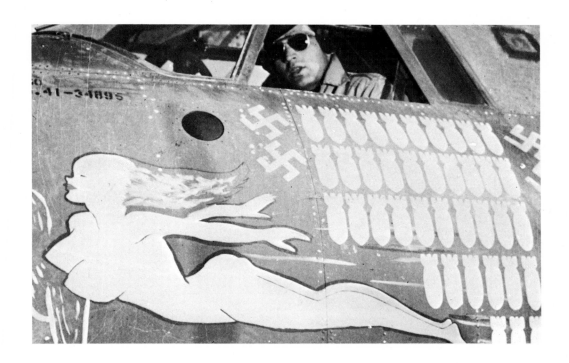

'Target For Tonight', section-B17 Flying Fortress (*CAF Collection*).

'Sweet & Lovely' B17 Flying Fortress, 8th AF England (*USAF*).

Above 'Miss Behave' P47 Thunderbolt (*USAF*). *Opposite* 'Mors Ab Alto' (Death from on High), section-B24 Liberator (*CAF Collection*).

MORS AB ALTO

Olsen

'Night Mission', section-B24 Liberator (*CAF Collection*).

'Anxious Angel', 91st BG B17 Flying Fortress, Bassingbourn, England 1944
(*Paul C Burnett*).

Above 'Strawberry Bitch' B24 Liberator (*USAF* Museum, Dayton, Ohio).
Opposite Varga's 'Torches At Midnight' pin-up (©1943 Esquire Inc.).

TORCHES AT MIDNIGHT

I guess he never knew how much I cared,
  For words of mine could never set it down . . .
It was a starlit time that we two shared
  The horns blew soft around the shadowed town . . .
I can remember ev'ry magic date,
  That velvet night we heard Sinatra sing . . .
Those breathless moments when I used to wait
  Just knowing that my telephone would ring;

And so like children on a flimsy throne
  We whiled away a drugged and dreamy reign
And now I carry on the game alone
  As rain beats down upon my windowpane . . .
Ours was the brightest, loveliest flame about—
How strange my tears should have to put it out!

**PAINTING BY VARGA
VERSE BY PHIL STACK**

Opposite above 'Our Baby' B24 Liberator, Pacific Theatre 1943 (*USAF*).
Opposite below 'Kuuipo' B24 Liberator, Pacific Theatre 1944 (*USAF*).
Above 'Miami Clipper', 91st BG B17 Flying Fortress, Bassingbourn, England 1944
(*Paul C Burnett*).

Above 'Surprise Attack', section-B24 Liberator (*CAF Collection*).
Opposite above 'Lassie I'm Home', section-B24 Liberator (*CAF Collection*).
Opposite below 'Innocent A Broad' B24 Liberator (*USAF*).

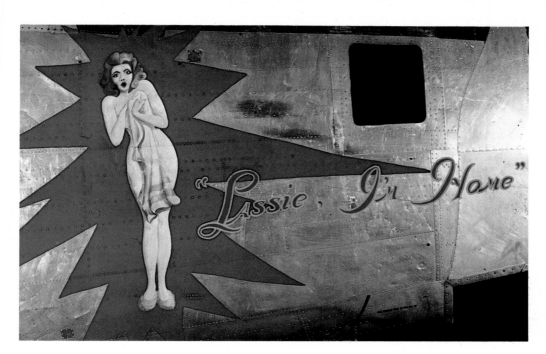

Opposite above 'Lady Helen of Wimpole', 91st BG Flying Fortress, Bassingbourn, England, 1944 (*Paul C Burnett*). *Opposite below* 'Ruby's Raiders' B17 Flying Fortress named after Cpl. Ruby Newell, winner of the 'Stars & Stripes' most beautiful WAC in England contest (*USAF*). *Above* B17 fragment (*CAF Collection*).

Opposite 'Ave Maria' B25 Mitchell, 12th AF, Italy (*USAF*).
Above 'Mutz', section-B17 Flying Fortress (*CAF Collection*).

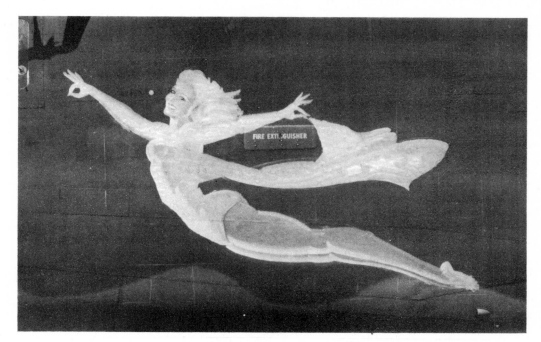

Opposite above 'Fiesty Sue' P51 Mustang (*USAF*). *Opposite left and right* Leather jackets worn by crew members of B17 Flying Fortresses 'Heavenly Body', and 'Mister Completely', 401st BG, 8th AF, England 1944 (*USAF*). *Above top* Pin-up painted on B24 Liberator (*USAF*). *Above* Varga's 'There'll Always Be A Christmas' pin-up (© 1943 Esquire Inc.).

'Mama Foo Foo', section-B24 Liberator (*CAF Collection*).

'Madame Shoo Shoo', 91st BG B17 Flying Fortress, Bassingbourn, England 1944
(*Paul C Burnett*).

Left 'Lady Grace' B24 Liberator, England 1944 (*USAF*). *Right* 'Off We Go' B24 Liberator, Pacific Theatre, 1945 (*USAF*).

'Home Stretch', section-B24 Liberator (*CAF Collection*).

'Squeeze', section-B24 Liberator (*CAF Collection*).

Pin-up, section-B24 Liberator (*CAF Collection*).

Above Rita Hayworth singing 'Put the Blame on Mame' from the 1940's film 'Gilda' (*National Film Archives*). *Opposite* 'Flamin' Mamie', section-B24 Liberator (*CAF Collection*).

PISTOL PACKIN' MAMA

The Wolves of the West
Lose a lot of their zest
  When this gun-totin' cutie is loose;
Their fervor is lackin',
Those rods she is packin'
  Can really be put into use!
Well, it's fun for a whirl
But "Arms and the Girl"
  Aren't a permanent part of her plan,
This Wild Prairie Blossom
Is just playin' possum
  And waitin' for Arms and THE MAN!

PAINTING BY VARGA
VERSE BY PHIL STACK

Above Varga's 'Pistol Packin Mama' pin-up (© *1944 Esquire Inc.*). *Opposite above*
'Fort Worth Gal' B17 Flying Fortress, Ridgewell, England 1944 (*USAF*).
Opposite below 'Baby Lou', 401st BG B17 Flying Fortress, England 1944 (*USAF*).

Opposite above 'Dragon Lady' B29 Superfortress, Korean War 1950-53.
Opposite below 'Dragon Lady' B24 Liberator, Guam, Marianas Islands, 1945 (*USAF*).
Above 'Yellow Fever', section-B24 Liberator (*CAF Collection*).

Above 'Miss Yourlovin', section-B24 Liberator (*CAF Collection*). *Opposite above*
'Little Gem' with artist, Ransdall W. Sprenger, 20th AF B29 Superfortress,
Saipan, Marianas Islands, 1945 (*USAF*). *Opposite below left* 'Wondrous Wanda'
B24 Liberator (*USAF*). *Opposite below right* Leather jacket worn by crew member
of B17 Flying Fortress 'Fancy Nancy', 401st BG, 8th AF, England 1944 (*USAF*).

Opposite 'The Outlaw' B29 Superfortress, Korean War, 1952-53. *Above* publicity
still from the film 'The Outlaw' starring Jane Russell (*National Film Archives*).

Above 'Nobby's Harriet 'Z', section-B17 Flying Fortress (*CAF Collection*).
Opposite above 'Lorilei' Douglas B26. *Opposite below* 'Sally B' B17 Flying Fortress
(*Euroworld Ltd., London*).

FEBRUARY

I'm learning some commando tricks.
For keeping fit, they're dandy,
And when you men come home again
They're apt to come in handy!

Above Varga's February 1944 pin-up (© *1943, Esquire Inc.*). *Opposite* 'Mount
N Ride', 91st BG Flying Fortress, Bassingbourn, England 1944 (*Joseph P Harlick*).

Opposite above 'Lonesome Lady' B24 Liberator (*USAF*). *Opposite below* 'Lucky Strike' B24 Liberator, Clarkfield, Phillipines, 1945 (*USAF*). *Above* 'Easy Maid', section-B24 Liberator (*CAF Collection*).

Opposite left 'Going My Way' B24 Liberator, Guam, Marianas Islands, 1945 (*USAF*).

Opposite right Leather jacket worn by crew member of B17 Flying Fortress
'Home James' 401st BG, 8th AF, England 1944 (*USAF*). *Above* 'Hikin' For
Home', 91st BG B17 Flying Fortress, Bassingbourn, England 1944 (*Paul C Burnett*).

Above 'Lucky Dog' B29 Superfortress, Korean War 1950-53. *Opposite above* 'Little Miss Mischief', 91st BG B17 Flying Fortress after belly landing at Bassingbourn, April 1945 (*USAF*). *Opposite below* 'Little Miss Mischief' in better shape . . . (*Paul C Burnett*).

'You Speak', section-B24 Liberator (*CAF Collection*).

'Forever Amber', section-B24 Liberator (*CAF Collection*).

Top 'Censored' B24 Liberator (*USAF*). *Below left* 'Censored' B24 Liberator,
Pacific Theatre 1944 (*USAF*). *Below right* 'Scrapiron IV', P38 Lightning 367th
FG, England 1944 (*USAF*). *Opposite above* 'Over Exposed' B24 Liberator,
Pacific Theatre, 1945 (*USAF*). *Opposite below* 'Photo Fanny' B24 Liberator, Pacific
Theatre, 1945 (*USAF*).

'Diamond Lil' B24 Liberator (*Confederate Airforce Museum*).

Left 'Fay' B29 Superfortress, 21st BC, Saipan, 1945 (*USAF*). *Right* 'Lassie Come Home', B29 Superfortress, 21st BC, Saipan 1945 (*USAF*).

LULLABY FOR A DREAM

As you go dreaming, save a dream for me,
  A dream of gay, inconsequential things,
When all we were to know was yet to be
  And young illusion colored all our springs;
Yes, while you dream, I hope that you recall
  A moon that dipped across an April sky . . .
That tiny inn we sought when night would fall . . .
  The candlelight . . . the wine . . . and You and I . . .

There is an end to laughter in the rain,
  There is an end to shadowed streets we knew,
Yet as the past cries out to me again
  It is a simple thing I ask of you:
As you go dreaming, save a dream for me . . .
Spun from the gossamer of used-to-be!

PAINTING BY VARGA—VERSE BY PHIL STACK

Above Varga's 'Lullaby For A Dream' pin-up (© 1941 *Esquire Inc.*).
Opposite above 'Next Objective' B29 Superfortress, New Mexico 1946 (*USAF*).
Opposite below 'You've Had It' B17 Flying Fortress, England, 1945 (*USAF*).

Opposite above 'The Wichita Witch' B29 Superfortress, 21st BC, Saipan, 1945
(*USAF*). *Opposite below* 'Glamouras' B24 Liberator, Phillipines, 1945 (*USAF*). *Above*
'Miss Barbara' 8th AF B17 Flying Fortress, England (*USAF*).

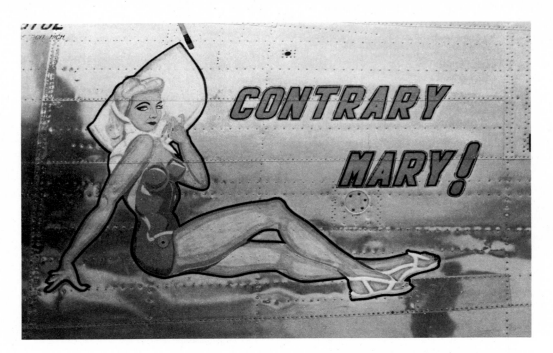

Top 'Contrary Mary' B24 Liberator (*USAF*). *Above left* 'Pugnacious Princess Pat' B24 Liberator (*USAF*). *Above right* Leather jacket worn by crew member of B17 Flying Fortress 'The Farmer's Daughter', 401st BG, 8th AF, England, 1945 (*USAF*). *Opposite above* 'Queenie', 91st BG B17 Flying Fortress, Bassingbourn, England (*Joseph P Harlick*). *Opposite below* 'Sweet Lorraine' B25 Mitchell, somewhere in India (*USAF*).

Above 'Sloppy But Safe', section-B24 Liberator (*CAF Collection*). *Opposite above* 'Our Gal' B24 Liberator (*USAF*). *Opposite left* 'Taylor Maid' B24 Liberator (*USAF*). *Opposite right* Leather jacket worn by crew member of B17 Flying Fortress, 'Miss B Haven', 401st BG, 8th AF, England 1944 (*USAF*).

Opposite above Honour roll of 350th Fighter Squardon, England 1945 (*USAF*).
Opposite below 533rd Bomb Squadron barber shop, England 1944 (*USAF*).
Above 'Delectable Doris' B24 Liberator, Duxford, England (*Yesterday's Airforce, California, USA*).

Above A-2 leather flying jacket of crew member and artist James Mountain. Girl depicted was his fiancé (*USAF Museum, Dayton, Ohio*). *Opposite* Leather jackets worn by crew members of B17 Flying Fortresses from 401st BG, 8th AF, England 1944-45 (*USAF*).

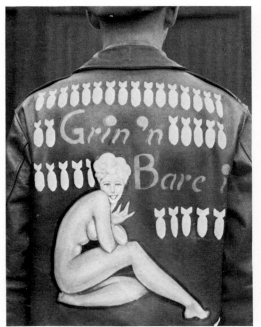

Opposite and above Leather jackets worn by crew members of B17 Flying Fortresses from 401st BG, 8th AF, England 1944-45 (*USAF*).

Left Cpl. Tony Starcer 91st BG resident artist painting B17 Flying Fortress
'General Ike' at Bassingbourn, England, 1944 (*Paul C Burnett*).
Right 1st Lt. George H Heilig in the cockpit of B17 Flying Fortress
'General Ike' (*USAF*).

Above top Ransdall W. Springer paints pin-up on Boeing B29 Superfortress, Saipan, Marianas Islands, 1944 (*USAF*).
Above left Artist painting B29 Superfortress pin-up (*USAF*).
Above right Cpl. Tony Starcer beside 91st BG Flying Fortress 'Heavyweight Annihilators No. 2' (*Paul C Burnett*).

Opposite above 'Toni C. II' Douglas B26, Pusan, Korea 1952 (*Robert C Mikesh*).
Opposite below 'Heart Breaking Kasha' Douglas B26, Pusan, Korea 1952 (*Robert C Mikesh*). *Above* 'Monie', Douglas B26 named after pilot Mikesh's wife Ramona, Pusan, Korea 1952 (*Robert C Mikesh*).

Top 'What Shebolians' Douglas B26, Pusan, Korea 1952 (*Robert C Mikesh*).
Above right 'Rice Paddy Wagon' Douglas B26, Korea 1952 (*Bruce Rigelsford*).
Opposite above 'L.S.M.F.C.' Douglas B26, Pusan, Korea 1952 (*Bruce Rigelsford*).
Opposite below 'Sweet Miss Lilian' Douglas B26, Pusan, Korea 1952 (*Bruce Rigelsford*).

'Pussy Galor' F105D Thunderchief painted and piloted by Capt. 'Vic' Viscarra over Vietnam (*Robert C Mikesh*). *Back cover* 'Mission Completed', section-B24 Liberator (*CAF Collection*).

Acknowledgements

Ian Logan and Henry Nield would like to thank everyone who has helped with the compilation of "Classy Chassy" but would particularly like to mention:
Major Richard E. Stevenson, of the Magazine & Book Branch Public Information Division, Secretary of the Air Force Office of Information, Pentagon, Washington D.C.;
Margaret B. Livesay, Walter Cate and Dana Bell of the Aerospace Audio-Visual Service, Arlington, Virginia;
Robert C. Mikesh, Associate Curator of Aeronautics, National Air & Space Museum, Smithsonian Institution, Washington, D.C.;
Royal Frey, Curator, and Charles Worman of the US Air Force Museum, Wright-Patterson Field, Dayton, Ohio;
Col. James P. Hill, Executive Director, Confederate Air Force, Rebel Field, Harlingen, Texas;
Phyllis Crawley, Director of Public Relations, Esquire Inc., New York;
also
Mr. & Mrs. P. C. Burnett of Aubern, Alabama and
Col., & Mrs. F. S. Kamykowski of Montgomery, Alabama, for their help and hospitality;
Benny, Carolyn, Ben & Courtney Kendrick, Arlington, Virginia, for their hospitality;
Roger Freeman, Joseph Harlick, Stephen Hudek, Ernest McDowell, David Menard, John Price and Bruce Riglesford;
finally
Roy Walker, book designer, for his patience and perseverance.